Dirty Diversity

A Practical Guide to Foster an Equitable and Inclusive Workplace for All

JANICE Z. GASSAM, PH.D.

Janice Z Gassam. © 2020

ISBN: 978-0-578-69716-1

Because of the dynamic nature of the internet, any web addresses or links contained in this book may have changed since publication and may no longer be valid. The views expressed in this work are solely those of the author and do not necessarily reflect the views of the publisher, and the publisher disclaims any responsibility for them.

Printed in the United States of America

www.drjanicegassam.com

Dedication

To my family:

Thank you Mom for all the sacrifices you have made on my behalf. You are such an inspiration to me, and I am so happy that God saw it fit for you to be my mother in this lifetime.

Thank you Dad for pushing me, GG, and CJ to value and cherish education and hard work. I guess I am following in your footsteps as a professor and now as an author. Watching you has inspired me in so many ways.

Thank you GG for being a great role model and inspiration to me in many ways.

Thank you CJ for providing support and encouragement always.

To my friends:

Thank you for your continued support and love. It does not go unnoticed.

To my husband:

Thank you for your patience and for always being there for me with support. Thank you for always listening to my corky ideas and for teaching me everything under the sun. Your encouragement and love are priceless, and you are the most amazing blessing in my life. I love you.

To Jasmine Womack:

Thank you for your guidance, patience, and kindness to help me write my first book. You are an amazing teacher, and I admire your journey. Keep shining and bringing more light into this world. You are making such an amazing impact.

CONTENTS

Introduction

Welcome! I am grateful you have trusted me to help you foster more inclusion and equity in your workplace. Organizations spend billions of dollars annually on diversity, equity and inclusion (DEI) initiatives and programs in the workplace. You are probably here because your organization has a DEI issue that you are trying to resolve. You may also be here because you are a DEI practitioner who wants to learn more about your craft. The reason why this book is called *Dirty Diversity* is because diversity has become a dirty word in the workplace and often brings about negative knee jerk reactions. Many people have become skeptical of the value of DEI despite existing research that indicates that greater diversity will lead to greater profits.

My hope is that through reading this book, you will uncover strategies for more inclusion, equity and belonging in your workplace. Being able to create an environment of inclusion will allow you to attract and retain diverse talent in your workplace. Readers will be given practical tips in this book for implementation. This book will help you understand how to implement different DEI strategies into the workplace, as well as methods that will propel your success.

In addition to consulting with over 30 organizations on different DEI issues, I have had the ability to study DEI at a deeper level and earned a Ph.D. in Applied Organizational Psychology. I have also had the opportunity to share my DEI insights in Forbes.com as a senior contributing writer and have written nearly 200 articles on several different aspects of DEI.

I have worked with Fortune 500 companies as well as non-profit organizations and institutions to deliver workshops around DEI. I have given keynote speeches on DEI to help spark important discussions within organizations. In 2018, I decided to create a consultancy, BWG Business Solutions, after realizing that there was a gap in the environment that leadership wants to foster compared to the culture that employees are actually experiencing. BWG stands for black, white, green. The main idea with the name is that diversity is not about black or white but about green, which is money. Companies that put a concerted effort into fostering equitable and inclusive environments where employees feel a sense of belonging will see greater profitability for the organization. I created something called the Diversity Dinner Dialogue (DDD), an informal event where people are invited to have critical conversations around DEI-related topics over food. Food is the great equalizer, and I realized that it is an effective tool to foster a safe environment in which difficult discourse could take place. Much of the insights in this book are from what I have learned through the DDD that I have facilitated in different cities around the United States.

One of my best experiences as a consultant occurred after my very first training. I received some critical feedback from attendees, and this information forced me to go back and research DEI more critically to refine my strategies and gain a deeper understanding of practical, effective implementations of DEI. At first, this negative feedback was a hard pill to swallow, but ultimately, feedback is one of the best tools for growth and innovation (as I will explain in more detail throughout this book). Through my consulting experiences as well as the DDD that I have hosted, I have learned an immense amount of information that I felt was imperative to share with the world and particularly with organizations that continuously struggle to retain diverse talent.

One of the biggest wins in my DEI career thus far was being contacted by well-known retail company H&M. In 2019, the company flew me out to Berlin, Germany and compensated me for taking part as a panel moderator for a discussion on diversity in the fashion industry. I was among global leaders in the company, fashion industry leaders, and international DEI changemakers. The fact that this international brand and company that I have supported as a consumer recognized my voice and my value and wanted me to take part in this global event is still mind-blowing. Their interest in my message on DEI let me know I was going in the right direction, and my contributions are impacting the world and the workplace.

The purpose of this book is simple. I want to help you infuse more love and understanding into the workplace. In this simple guide, I will give you practical steps to establish more equity and inclusion in your workplace based on my experiences as a DEI practitioner and the research I've conducted. This is a book for managers, DEI practitioners and employees hoping to create a more equitable workplace. I encourage you to read this book with a highlighter and take notes on how these strategies can be applied directly into your workplace.

I am here with you on your journey to creating a more love-filled work culture; congratulations on taking this step to improve your company's health!

SECTION 1

FOR MANAGERS

CHAPTER 1

Reducing Microaggressions

Hello Boss! Welcome to the journey. This section is divided into five chapters that focus on the most important strategies you can utilize to create a diverse, equitable and inclusive workplace. Research indicates that inclusion and belonging have changed vastly in the workplace compared to decades ago. Discrimination has completely morphed and changed in today's workplaces. The research demonstrated that much of the biased behaviors that occur currently in the workplace are covert behaviors. Microaggressive behaviors have become more common in today's workplaces. Microaggressions are hostile words or behaviors that unintentionally or intentionally make marginalized groups feel excluded. It can be things like being ignored by coworkers, being left off an email chain or given more work on a particular project. It could also manifest as being talked over during a boardroom meeting or being labeled as less qualified than peers. On the surface the receiver may question whether they are being treated differently than others, but over time microaggressions can have a detrimental effect on employees and the organizational culture at large.

Research indicates that one of the most effective ways to address microaggressive behaviors is a strategy called Management By Walking Around (MBWA) (Phipps & Prieto, 2016). The theory behind this is that managers who are frequently around the employees they manage are better able to spot and manage the more benign behaviors, thus preventing the more egregious conduct from occurring. The main idea behind MBWA is that by walking around more frequently, managers are better able to recognize and address smaller problems in their organizations to prevent these from becoming more significant issues in the future. If the smaller behaviors like microaggressions are addressed in an effective and timely manner, companies can prevent some of the larger and more overt discriminatory behaviors from taking place in the workplace.

I've had managers who were more active and involved managers. At first, I did not like their management style because I greatly enjoyed autonomy in my roles. However, having a more active manager helped me feel connected to my workplace. While many people do not share the same sentiments with me about active managers and may disagree with me about the benefits of having one, being more active and involved in what's going on with your employees will allow you to recognize when problems arise. Having a manager who is disconnected from the employees will not create a sense of belonging or family among the employees in the organization.

One of the problematic aspects of microaggressions is that they are often invisible, and when explained to somebody else, they may sound harmless. Sometimes people feel it may not be a big deal. I once heard microaggressions being described as death by a thousand cuts, and to this day, I still use that image as a way to illustrate the effects of microaggressions over time. One microaggression is not going to be the end all, be all, but it's the continued microaggressive behaviors and statements that can leave an employee feeling depleted and can impact his or her sense of inclusion and belonging. Policies, procedures and protocol for addressing microaggressions should be introduced. Consider also including microaggression training for employees to get them familiar with recognizing and dealing with microaggressive behaviors. Creating clear lines of communication for managers and employees is so vital for your DEI efforts. For employees who work in remote settings or in settings where they do not see their managers on a frequent basis, phone and video conferences are effective ways for managers to make their presence felt, which can allow managers to be better able to recognize and address discriminatory behaviors when they occur.

Chapter Takeaways:

- Microaggressions have become more common in today's workplaces.

- Managers who are more active and present among employees are better able to recognize discriminatory behavior.

- Include microaggression training into your workplace to equip employees with the tools to navigate these behaviors.

CHAPTER 2

What Drives Employee Belonging?

I remember starting a job with the same credentials that everyone else had, but my employer never put my name on my office door. I was on a completely different floor than my colleagues. When people came looking for me, they didn't know which one was my office because they never bothered to put my name on the door. In addition, management rarely came to visit my office to see how I was doing and how I was acclimating to my new role. Ernst & Young recently came out with something called the Belonging Barometer (Twaronite, 2019). Based on their research, they found that one of the best ways to foster belonging among employees is regular manager check-ins.

These could be daily or even weekly check-ins to assess how employees are doing.

Managers should be doing check-ins on a consistent basis with employees. If possible, it's best for check-ins to take place in person. Check-ins could also take place via email when a manager reaches out to an employee to see how he or she is doing. Check-ins could look like a virtual coffee meeting where a leader reaches out via video chat using a platform like Zoom. For an in-person check-in, a manager should visit an employee's office to see how he or she is doing. Managers can ask questions about how work-related tasks are coming along or how the team dynamics are. Managers can also ask employees about how they're feeling, how their day is going and how their families are doing.

Thinking back, I worked in an organization in which I didn't even realize that I was receiving frequent check-ins from both my managers and some of my colleagues. My colleagues went out of their way to introduce themselves to me during my first year at that organization, and they made sure that I knew who they were. Their efforts made me feel like I was part of their team, and although I was the only black woman in the department, they made me feel like I was part of a family. This was a really effective way to create a sense of belonging for me.

If you are a manager, a small yet effective tip is to take note of the details about employees and co-workers and add that information to your check-ins. If an employee shares that a family member is sick, when you check in with the employee, it's encouraging to ask about the family member and assess how that person is doing. I'm not always one who remembers every single detail, so my best friend has become the Notes app on my phone. I write down notes about everything, and I keep them in case I ever need to refer back to them. If you don't remember details, write a note in your phone and then set a reminder for yourself to go back to that information. Check-ins are an integral part of creating a sense of inclusion and belonging for employees in your workplace.

Chapter Takeaways:

- Think about how often you are checking in and checking up on employees.

- Check-ins are best when they are done in person, but they can be done virtually.

- Check-ins should be done on a frequent and ongoing basis to drive belonging.

CHAPTER 3

Are Panel Discussions and Focus Groups Worthwhile?

On LinkedIn a few years ago, I saw a flyer for an event that was a panel discussion about the politics of black women's hair. I thought that the panel idea was amazing. The tickets actually sold out, and I was a bit upset because I didn't get an opportunity to take part in the discussion. The discussion was taking place at a well-known company's office in New York City. As a black woman, it was a refreshing feeling to see such a critical discussion taking place because it's not something I see often happening in the corporate space. I thought that it would be amazing to be part of an organization that was as forward thinking as that one. When these types of discussions take place, it lets employees of all backgrounds feel seen. If I were part of this organization, it would have strengthened my sense of belonging.

Having a conversation related to the issues faced by different groups can foster feelings of inclusion. Conducting panel discussions focused on topics that are of value to me showed me the importance of panels, which are sometimes overlooked in corporate DEI efforts. Outside of Women's History Month, Black History Month, and Hispanic Heritage Month, organizations have an underutilized opportunity to have critical conversations without expending a lot of money. It's important to utilize a multi-pronged approach to DEI and have multiple ways to elicit DEI discussions.

Last year, well-known fashion retailer H&M brought me in to moderate a panel with their global leadership and DEI catalysts from around the world. This panel discussion was focused on strategies to create more diversity and inclusion within the fashion industry. During the discussion, we focused on ways that fashion retailers can be more inclusive when creating and marketing products. We also discussed the importance of receiving feedback from a diverse group of individuals before launching an ad campaign. In addition, strategies to create more diversity within fashion schools was a topic that was highlighted during the discussion. Despite past controversy in which the company was embroiled, I thought that the panel was a really great way to show employees and customers that the company was really trying to make an effort to change the narrative and create more inclusive products as well as a more equitable fashion industry.

Panel discussions are a very inexpensive way to help employees feel a sense of connection, inclusion and belonging within their organization. In many of the panel discussions in which I have participated, panelists are offering their time and energy as a complimentary service for the organization. Companies that have lots of office space can benefit greatly from panel discussions because they can partner with small organizations or DEI-focused non-profit organizations to host panel discussions in their space. This is a win-win for both the smaller organization, your company, and your employees. Ask employees what topics they would enjoy discussing more frequently and bring in subject matter experts in those particular topic areas to just come and speak with and engage with employees. You could also invite speakers to come and give keynote talks. Lunch and learns are becoming a very popular method for DEI discussions, as well.

Panels are an effective way to build a sense of belonging. Black employees, for example, will feel a sense of belonging if their organization creates events around issues that are unique to them. Inviting others to engage in these discussions to learn more is a necessary component when you are striving to foster more inclusion and belonging. Many of the DEI issues organizations face are caused by a lack of knowledge and understanding that people have about other cultures. A lot of companies talk the talk, but they do not walk the walk. A disturbing pattern I have noticed is that women-centered events, for example, are only taking place during Women's History Month. If you truly value your female employees, host women-centered events outside of Women's History Month. What you want to do is ensure that there is continued communication and conversation around DEI whether that's through panel discussions, talks, or focus groups. You want to keep the dialogue going because that is what's really going to impact your DEI efforts. Throughout my DEI career, I've been asked to take part in several panels at many different organizations. I find that panels are a really effective way to show employees that the company is making a concerted effort to foster deeper understanding.

Another way to strengthen your DEI efforts is via focus groups. Focus groups can consist of DEI change-makers within the organization, those who are passionate about DEI, or members of a particular demographic. The focus group can conduct a discussion of a particular DEI issue with group members of diverse opinions and can function as a think-tank that strategizes how that issue can be resolved. Rather than the DEI responsibilities falling on one person such as a chief diversity officer or diversity head, the DEI focus group can be a more impactful way to help you reach your DEI objectives. A focus group may be thought of as similar to a diversity task force. It is simply a group of individuals within the organization who come together to ponder and share their feedback and opinions about a particular DEI-related issue. Implementing focus groups into your organization can help you better understand your DEI issues and come up with effective solutions.

Chapter Takeaways:

- Panel discussions are a great way to have conversations in which subject matter experts share their knowledge and expertise with employees.

- Panel discussions are a low-cost way to foster inclusion by highlighting topics employees care about.

- Focus groups can be used to solicit DEI-related information that will help address DEI issues.

CHAPTER 4

The Importance of the
Feedback Loop

It is frequently said that what gets measured gets improved, and in DEI, that statement is 100% accurate. What gets measured on a consistent and ongoing basis is what gets improved. Consistent feedback leads to improved performance and this can be helpful to achieve corporate DEI objectives. Employers have a wide array of feedback from employees. Exit interview data for example, is a great source of information for employers. Many companies conduct exit interviews when employees leave their organization. Sometimes, the interviews are conducted in person, and other times they are conducted over the phone or online. Another source of employee feedback is the contents of an employee resignation letter. It can contain vital and pertinent information and feedback for the organization.

You want to ensure that your company has a continuous feedback loop. A feedback loop is an ongoing process where communication and feedback can take place. A company with a continuous feedback loop will be better able to understand and assess DEI-related issues when they emerge. The feedback loop is necessary for any sort of DEI efforts your company engages in. Whether you are aware of it or not, you are continuously receiving feedback from employees that can help you improve your organization's DEI efforts. Organizations should offer multiple methods for employees to give feedback on a consistent and ongoing basis. Aside from the most popular feedback method, which is surveys, online reviews and exit interviews can be assessed and 360-degree feedback systems should be implemented to strengthen the feedback loop.

When I was working in the banking industry, I ended up leaving my organization because it became too much for me to juggle graduate school full-time and work 40 hours a week. I decided to resign from my position. When I resigned, I was asked to complete an exit interview by phone. I also gave my notice via a letter in which I outlined all my grievances and explained in detail how I came to my decision. In the letter, I offered advice to the company on how to strengthen employee relations. A Harvard Business Review study found that about 75% of companies surveyed conducted some type of exit interviews. Exit interview data is a prime location for you to go to assess, understand and diagnose your organization's DEI issues and determine what needs to be fixed (Spain & Groysberg, 2016). Be sure that you are assessing exit interview information. This can be done through a textual analysis. This would require the verbal feedback from former employees to be transcribed and then an analysis can be done of both this transcribed information as well as any written feedback former employees have left, to assess whether there are recurring themes that emerge. Once themes are identified, solutions can be developed.

It's also important to understand that there is a vast amount of feedback that is available online. The online feedback that is available can help you gauge the corporate culture of inclusion (or exclusion). It is good just to be aware of some of the resources that are available to you. If you go and search your company's name on a website that reviews companies and includes employee testimonials, you can find positive and negative experiences from employees. If your company is a well-known company, you are likely to find a plethora of reviews from past and current employees. The feedback is a great indicator of the culture within the organization although you want to consider the fact that people are more likely to write negative feedback online than they are to share positive feedback. If you see recurring themes in the online feedback, this can give you some valuable insights and be an indication of some underlying DEI issues that your organization is facing.

Another recommendation I would make is a 360-degree feedback system that is specific to DEI. A 360-degree feedback system is a method utilized by organizations to get feedback from every level of an organization including management reviews, peer reviews, and self-assessments. A 360-degree feedback system is not a system that I have ever seen used for DEI, but it can be an effective way to gain priceless feedback. As a manager, you are creating a culture of inclusion. Ponder whether employees are creating a culture of belonging. In addition, consider what you have done to foster inclusion for your coworkers. Soliciting feedback on a continuous and ongoing basis is going to be what propels your organization forward in your DEI efforts.

Chapter Takeaways:

- There are several different ways that organizations can assess feedback from employees, which includes online reviews and exit interview information.

- Feedback loops will help your organization determine and understand what areas of DEI should be its focus.

- 360-degree feedback can be an effective system to receive constructive feedback from a variety of sources that will help your organization improve DEI efforts.

CHAPTER 5

Fostering Inclusion and Equity for Remote Workers

In 2020, the novel coronavirus altered and completely transformed the world as we know it today. Many people started working remotely from home. The global pandemic altered the landscape of the workplace and organizations for what may be the indefinite future. In remote work, it is more important than ever to create and foster a sense of belonging for employees. A few years ago I was an instructor at a university and I developed and taught classes in a purely online format. My experience as a remote/online professor taught me a lot about what is necessary to create belonging.

During the 2020 global pandemic, more and more companies are conducting weekly or even daily virtual check-ins to strengthen that sense of inclusion that is often lost in purely remote settings. It is important that you build into your organization different ways to connect, and it is imperative that as a manager, you create ways for your team to forge bonds as a community such as informally meeting with an employee virtually for coffee or lunch meetings, or more formal meetings. Virtual meetings should be embedded into the fabric of the organization. If the Covid-19 pandemic taught the world anything, it is the importance of creating and setting up systems conducive to an online and virtual format. Be sure to ask your employees what their preferred method of communication is. The go-to for many organizations is video conferencing but for several different reasons, employees may not want to turn their video feature on. If employees prefer other methods of communication like email, phone calls or text, be sure to utilize these. There is no one-size-fits-all communication style for employees.

Frequent meetings are absolutely necessary. As previously indicated, check-ins are extremely effective at creating a sense of belonging and are perhaps even more essential for team members who work remotely. You can ask employees to share food that they're eating or the recipes that they're trying with their team members every week. Different employees can share dishes that they enjoy or are from their native country. You could also have an MTV Cribs-style virtual tour in which employees show part of their home for their colleagues or give them a refrigerator tour. You could create a cloud-based employee playlist (Spotify is great) that each employee can edit; this is a really cool way to share music that means a lot to you and allows others into your world. There are several different ways to create inclusion amongst remote workers. Your company just has to be creative when doing it. It's a good idea to establish guidelines for these creative bonding activities so that there is more structure and clarity and also to ensure that these are activities that employees are comfortable with participating in. Ultimately, employees want to feel a sense of belonging, and building community is one of the most effective ways to do that in your workplace.

Chapter Takeaways:

- Frequently checking in with remote employees is an effective way to foster inclusion and belonging.

- There are several creative ways to foster belonging for remote workers including sharing recipes and playlists.

- Creating multiple ways to connect and build community is a strategy that will strengthen company culture even after the impacts of Covid-19 have ceased.

SECTION 2

FOR DEI
PRACTITIONERS

CHAPTER 6

Read This Before Implementing a Workshop or Training Program

You are reading this section because you are a DEI consultant or aspiring consultant who wants to strengthen your DEI workshops and training programs. As you may already know from being a DEI practitioner, the workshops and trainings are like the spices that make the food taste good. Think about how bland the food would taste without any spices. That is how vital workshops and trainings are for organizational DEI efforts.

My primary role as a DEI consultant has been administering, delivering and facilitating different workshops and trainings for organizations: it is the bread and butter of my DEI efforts. I've been able to work with a number of small and large companies as well as universities, institutions, and nonprofits. I've received a considerable amount of feedback from my training experiences. The majority of the work I do is in designing and developing workshops and trainings that address particular DEI issues a company is facing. This section will focus on what I have learned thus far regarding how to structure your workshops and training programs for success.

An external consultant is normally someone who either a) works for an outside organization, or b) works as an independent contractor through his or her own consultancy. External consultants are frequently called on to design and implement DEI workshops and training programs. An alternative that organizations sometimes use is a chief diversity officer or diversity head who designs workshops and training programs. There are a number of different reasons why external consultants are highly effective at conducting these workshops and trainings. One reason is that external consultants are more objective. As an external consultant, we are able to take the feedback we receive after a workshop or training and use it to refine future workshops and trainings. There is a more refined set of skills that an external consultant possesses, which are helpful especially when a company is dealing with more complex DEI issues.

One of the very first DEI workshops that I conducted was centered around cultural competency and communication. This experience was my very first time delivering a workshop, and I was very nervous. It was a three-hour workshop for a non-profit organization for its annual all-hands meeting. There were about 30 to 40 people who were present in the training. During the training, there was a series of activities that I had planned for the attendees based on what the client's specific needs were. Initially, when I got to the training location, there were two other trainings taking place simultaneously in the rooms next to where our training session was located, so the attendees could not hear what I was saying. I had a PowerPoint presentation set up and because of the noise levels, we had to transition to a different location in the building. I ended up having to modify the activities that were planned.

In the initial call I had with the client, the DEI issues had not been articulated to me in detail. That particular situation taught me about the importance of the discovery call and how imperative it is for DEI professionals to dig deep during this call in order to properly diagnose the specific DEI issues that an organization is facing. Following the workshop, the employees left some critical feedback, with complaints about the value of some activities we did, and some questions about the relevance of the activities to the specific DEI issues the company was facing. As devastating as the critical feedback was, it helped strengthen my abilities as a DEI consultant.

The main takeaways from this particular incident were vast. The discovery call is imperative when conducting workshops and trainings as a DEI consultant. A discovery call will help you as a DEI practitioner understand and uncover the DEI issues faced by the company so that you can craft effective solutions. Rather than expecting organizational leaders to provide you with the information needed to adequately diagnose the issues, coming up with some questions beforehand to uncover these particular issues is vital. Asking not only about what the specific DEI issues are but how long the company has been facing these issues, what implementations have been conducted in the past and possible predictions as to why the implementations were ineffective is crucial.

They say the best predictor of future behavior is past behavior. When a potential client reaches out about a DEI workshop or training, have discussions with the organization about past habits. What I often learn through this initial discovery call is that I am being brought in for the very first time to an organization and that the company has never done a workshop or DEI training before. What has become extremely apparent is that companies need to invest more time and resources into DEI trainings and workshops.

Not only did I learn the importance of the discovery call but I also learned that DEI trainings and workshops will often lose their structure so as a facilitator it's important to have an outline of topics you want to cover but be open to the possibility of every activity and discussion not fitting into the time allotted. Create a list of the main issues the company is facing and which of the activities included will address each of these specific issues. DEI practitioners must prepare for any and every situation. If the technology is not working, be prepared to do your presentation without it.

Based on my experiences, 70% of companies do not conduct DEI workshops and trainings on a regular basis or more than once a year. This is a practice that needs to stop if companies want to create a workplace that is inclusive and fosters a sense of belonging. It's really interesting to think that so many companies are not doing DEI workshops and trainings on a consistent basis. If harassment training is required annually, why isn't the same true for DEI training? My recommendation would be to encourage companies to conduct some sort of DEI workshop or training every month. This can be held virtually or in-person and can cover different DEI-related topics. What is important is that the conversation is continued and does not stop with the annual or one-time-only bias training. Express to the organizations you work with the value of consistent and ongoing DEI workshops and trainings.

Lastly, as an external consultant, it is important to keep records of all of the organizations and institutions you have worked with, as well as the feedback you receive. When companies reach out to you to enlist your services, they will ask for recommendations and references. Think about who can speak highly of your work, your skills and your expertise. Keep records of these individuals and institutions in which your DEI workshops and training programs have been successful (based on management and employee feedback). Also try to take note of which facets of the workshop have led to success, so you can use these strategies for continued success in the future. Keep records of which workshop/training strategies you have implemented that have not been effective and be sure to uncover why they were ineffective so you can improve the quality of your efforts moving forward.

Chapter Takeaways:

- Discovery calls are vital when conducting DEI workshops and training sessions.

- Organizations do not conduct DEI workshops and training programs frequently. Emphasize to management the importance of ongoing training.

- As a DEI consultant, be ready to pivot in any situation the day of a workshop or training session.

- Be sure to keep records from all your workshops and training sessions for future reference.

CHAPTER 7

Crafting Effective DEI Workshops and Training Programs

I have found that scenario-based activities have been really effective in my workshops and training sessions. My positive experiences with scenario-based activities are supported by research. The evidence indicates that when you are conducting DEI workshops and training, scenario-based activities based on real work situations are effective. These activities are relevant to what employees actually may experience in the workplace. As I reflect on the story that I shared about the very first workshop that I ever conducted, at the very end of that workshop, I included an activity on microaggressions. In the activity, I separated the attendees into different groups, and each group was supposed to discuss how to resolve a particular microaggression issue. Each group was instructed to read a brief description of the behavior and then discuss with their group members what the best course of action would be to handle that behavior. After participants had an opportunity to discuss their thoughts (I gave them about ten minutes) we reconvened as a group.

I really enjoyed this activity, and it was clear that the attendees did as well, but I conducted the activity at the very end of the workshop, so we ran out of time. Only two thirds of the participants were able to share their groups' insights. Based on their feedback, the attendees really seemed to enjoy the activity and wished that they had more time to discuss these microaggressive behaviors and strategies to handle them with not only their group members but also with the rest of their colleagues in the larger group. Scenario-based activities work most effectively to illustrate these difficult-to-discuss points when it comes to DEI. Workshops should be full of scenario-based activities that attendees talk through and work through either individually or with teams. These activities should encourage the participants to discuss and decide what the best courses of action are to deal with specific behaviors.

In the past, I conducted a webinar for a public school system. According to the human resource department, one of the problems that the school district was facing was an inability to hire and retain teachers of color. This was problematic because the students in the district were mostly students of color. During the webinar that I conducted for them, I gave very specific scenarios that were common within organizations that were unable to attract and retain diverse talent. This is a very common DEI issue that is faced by organizations large and wide. I shared with attendees some of the ways to resolve this issue, including diversifying their pipeline, ensuring the search committees are diverse and conducting DEI training for the school board members. I offered scenarios from past companies I have worked with and shared how they have been able to increase and retain diverse talent. After I assessed the feedback that I received following the webinar, it was apparent that one aspect that the attendees enjoyed from the workshop was the specific scenarios related to their DEI issues. When you're crafting a workshop, it's vital to include relevant scenario-based activities.

Timing and Size of Workshops and Training Sessions

When you're conducting DEI workshops, it's important to consider the timing of the workshop.

From past workshops, I've learned that it's always vital to think about the length of the workshop, the time that the workshop will actually take place, and the day of the week. All of these factors can impact how effective a workshop actually is for attendees. As you work with organizations, make an effort to optimize these aspects of the workshop for quality assurance.

Every company is different, so I would encourage you to ask leadership the following questions: 1) Are your employees most productive in the morning, afternoon, or evening? 2) In what setting will the workshop be held? A lecture and classroom format may work well if there is a one-way dialogue that must take place. If you want to give employees foundational information about a topic through definitions, concepts and theories, a traditional classroom setting may work best.

As far as timing, what I have found in my experiences is that there is a sweet spot between the late morning and early afternoon. Tuesdays and Wednesdays between 11:00 AM and 1:00 PM are the best days and times to hold a training session. I don't know why, but this window seems to be a great time slot to conduct workshops. 11:00 AM is not too early in the morning and 1:00 PM is a good time because it is just after lunch and right before attendees hit that mid-afternoon slump. It's important to note, though, that this holds true for U.S.-based companies and will vary vastly based on the culture of different countries and corporations. I would encourage you to take timing into consideration when conducting workshops to ensure attendees are focused and attentive.

In addition to timing, I would recommend DEI workshop and training session length to be kept under three hours. Anything beyond three hours may be overwhelming for participants. If there is a lot of information that must be covered, it is ideal to break the information up into digestible pieces. A DEI workshop should be broken up into multiple sessions in order to cover multiple topics and issues. Three hours per day is optimal.

In my experiences, the ideal in-person workshop size is about 20-30 people. More than 30 people in a workshop will make it more challenging for the participants to be able to have in-depth discussions. I always recommend breaking the group up if it is larger than 30 people. Because of the nature of these discussions, smaller group sizes also allow for a greater sense of community and afford each person the opportunity to be candid. It is challenging for individual involvement to take place in larger groups exceeding 30 people. In a 200 group session, only a fraction of the attendees would be able to contribute to the discussion. Smaller groups also allow for more intimate discussions to take place.

Focus

Workshop topics are a vastly important issue to take into consideration. Do not shy away from controversial topics. I want to see more companies putting an emphasis on discussions about race because what I've found is that race is one of, if not *the* most difficult thing for people to talk about in DEI workshops. In my experience, I've noticed that there is more ease when discussing topics like gender. Gender is not a difficult subject to discuss because everyone has someone of a different gender in their life. Race, on the other hand, is challenging because many people live in insular environments where they have little to no contact with those of other races.

A few years ago, I was on a consultation call with two different people from an organization who wanted me to come in and conduct a DEI workshop. On that consultation call with the client, one of the representatives from the organization explicitly stated that they did not want me to have discussions about things like white privilege and racism during the workshop. I found that to be interesting because it was an unconscious bias workshop that I was being asked to conduct. Understanding how things like power, race, and privilege can impact our decisions and give us different advantages or disadvantages is a really important aspect of understanding when examining unconscious bias; the directive from the representatives was problematic. I ended up designing the workshop to include only subtle mentions of these "forbidden" topics, without using the specified language that the client did not want included. My understanding was that the particular verbiage is triggering and would have made employees less receptive to the message, which is why the client was requesting these topics be excluded from the workshop.

I find that the popular topics that organizations want me to come in and talk about include topics that are less controversial. Some of these topics are things like emotional intelligence and navigating a toxic workplace. In 2017, I gave a TEDx talk on emotional intelligence and it has become a highly-requested workshop topic for me. Some of these more difficult-to-digest topics such as how to facilitate racial dialogue, topics around race and issues of perceived white privilege are more difficult subjects to chew on, and oftentimes, organizational leaders steer DEI workshops and trainings away from these areas.

Skirting around critical issues will not fix DEI problems; it's vital that any sort of DEI objectives and initiatives dig deeply. An essential aspect of DEI is digging deep and really assessing things without rose-colored glasses. It's important that companies aren't afraid to discuss controversial topics during their DEI efforts. DEI consultants should emphasize this to management. Workshops should center around some of these more difficult issues because the more they shy away from talking about them, the longer those problems will persist within the workplace.

Chapter Takeaways:

- Scenario-based activities should be used for workshops and training sessions.

- Workshops and training sessions should be between 1-3 hours long and should take place in the middle of the work day.

- Keeping your workshops and training sessions to no more than 30 people is ideal.

- Encourage organizations to explore more challenging topics for DEI workshops and training sessions.

CHAPTER 8

The Value of the Diversity Dinner Dialogue

In February 2019, I decided to create something called the Diversity Dinner Dialogue (DDD) through my consultancy, BWG Business Solutions. I decided to create the DDD because I recognized that people needed an outlet to talk with other people about DEI issues in an informal way. When I moved to New York, I was really interested in the DEI space, and I was trying to enter into that arena. I attended so many different panels and networking events. I joined groups that were centered around DEI in New York City and what I noticed was that, after DEI panel discussions, it was so hard to connect with the speakers. I also found it difficult to connect with other aspiring DEI professionals and changemakers even though these events were being advertised as networking events. I decided to create what I felt was missing in the DEI space.

One of the reasons why I was going to these panels was to network. I wanted to network with both novices like myself and leaders who were trailblazers in the DEI industry. What I noticed was that the panels consisted of a discussion on things that I somewhat already knew through my studies and research. People wanted a very low-stakes, informal, and safe environment to just discuss their DEI issues. I realized that although panels do have a lot of value for employees and attendees, I was not able to forge the connections I was hoping for through those panel discussions. Panels are extremely valuable for discussions where the panelists, who are typically subject matter experts, share their knowledge and expertise. As discussed above, panels should be part of your DEI strategy, but there's also a lot of value in having an open dialogue, where participants play an active role in the conversation. I created the DDD for that two-way conversation. I facilitate discussions on topics like allyship, hair discrimination, intersectionality, diverse leadership barriers, and gender equity. Through LinkedIn, I have received a barrage of suggestions for upcoming DDD events.

What I found in the DDD is that people really, really enjoy the food aspect, and I believe that DEI efforts should include food for the participants to keep them engaged. Hear me out. I know it sounds kind of funny, but food really is the great equalizer. Food helps to bond people, and it helps people open up. Why is that? Well, everybody needs to eat, and we all have things that we love to eat. We all have things that we don't love to eat, and food is a great way to just bring people together. If we have different political views, have different religious backgrounds, or are from different races, if you like macaroni and cheese, and I like macaroni and cheese, that's one thing that we have in common. Companies should really focus on having difficult dialogue over food (I'm partial to pizza), but you want to have a diversity of food choices as well to account for different food preferences. I suggest having a different variety of food choices that are easy to eat and are not messy. Messier foods make it difficult to engage in conversations while eating. Having and creating a way to have informal dialogue is critical in your DEI efforts.

Popular pizza company Papa John's took notice of my DEI efforts and the model of feeding participants that I was using and decided to sponsor the DDD. The DDD became a safe space to discuss, over delicious pizza, really difficult issues that employees and DEI professionals were facing. The DDD was really about creating informal opportunities for dialogue around DEI to take place. I've taken part in many DEI events both in-person and online. The key ingredient to the success of the DDD is that it is not taped or recorded. I attempted to record one of the first DDDs and forgot to start my live stream. Ironically, it was a blessing that the recording did not work because attendees shared with me that they were nervous about being on camera, and that being filmed or live streamed would take away the authenticity of the DDD. The safe space that is created in the DDD allows attendees to feel comfortable. One of the shining moments of the DDD occurred when one attendee felt comfortable sharing experiences with a gender transition. During the DDD attendees feel comfortable sharing their vulnerabilities because I make it a point to share my own flaws, biases and blindspots. I think this sharing of vulnerabilities allows others to feel comfortable being transparent and sharing their experiences.

One other important consideration should be the seating arrangement. In a room with tables and chairs, the default setting is having the speaker or facilitators at the front and lining the chairs up in rows and columns that mimic a typical classroom setting. To create a safe space, I would advise against this set up. Putting the chairs in a square or a circle is a minor change, yet immensely effective in promoting equity and inclusion. No one person is more of an authority figure than another. Each person's contributions are as valuable as the next person's contributions. You are creating an environment in which attendees can share what they're going through and have support from their peers. If you are able to create this sort of community within your organization, employees will be more likely to open up and to share their thoughts and their experiences.

Chapter Takeaways:

- Introducing a Diversity Dinner Dialogue-like event into your organization can help you foster more inclusion.

- Food is a great way to bond people, especially when engaging in difficult dialogue.

- Vulnerability is an important aspect of DEI-related conversations.

SECTION 3

FOR EMPLOYEES

CHAPTER 9

When You Don't See Eye to Eye

Think back to a time when you were having a discussion with someone with whom you didn't see eye to eye. It may be someone who had divergent political views from yours or somebody you were debating in regards to a law, morality or even religious beliefs. Think about how frustrating it is when you're having a conversation with someone who is simply not listening to you. You may feel like you're just talking to a wall, or the person is talking over you, and everything you're saying to that person is going in one ear and out another. You're not making any headway in the discussion. Increasing the opportunities for employees to have conversations may also increase the opportunity for misunderstandings to take place. There should be a system in place for dealing with misunderstandings and miscommunication. This chapter will focus on some different ways that you can address interpersonal issues you may have with coworkers.

I think back to many years ago when I was having a conversation with a white male friend who didn't understand the concept of white privilege. He didn't feel like he was privileged because he came from more modest means, and when he was growing up, his family did not have a lot of money. He wanted to understand better why white privilege was a thing because he didn't feel like race made somebody more privileged or less privileged than another person. We had a really great discussion, and he said he learned a lot through that conversation. I was able to listen to his perspective and offer my perspective on privilege and how it can manifest in different ways. I think he had never really engaged in an honest conversation about privilege prior to that discussion but being able to have the conversation helped him understand things a bit differently.

What made that conversation so impactful is that I was able to listen without responding and without the intention to respond. I was trying to listen for the purpose of understanding. Many times, we listen, but as we're listening, we're formulating a response in our head. Think about how much better our discussions would be if we were listening to understand the other person's point of view. If you go into a conversation assuming that you will never understand the point of view of the person with whom you are talking, your perception is your reality, and you're not going to understand that person, and perhaps, that person is not going to understand you. If, on the other hand, you enter into a discussion with the intention to understand the person, that perspective can shift the entire conversation. One trick I learned that I implement in discussions in which I don't see eye to eye with the other person is the 5-second rule. With this rule, you wait at least five seconds after a person finishes talking before responding to them. We all have a natural human tendency to want to react, oftentimes before fully thinking through what the person said and before properly articulating a response based on our understanding. The 5-second rule is a great practice to implement in the workplace and when having difficult discussions. The exercise forces one to listen before responding, which many of us don't do when we are engaged in a conversation. Simply being able to fully listen before responding can greatly improve the quality of our communication.

I think back to another time when I was having a discussion with a close friend. The friend had used the word 'nappy' to refer to a popular singer's hair. I have always found the term offensive since it is almost exclusively used to describe black hair that is seen as unruly and unkempt. During the conversation, I felt myself getting frustrated. After my friend made the statement, I explained to him my disdain for the word and why I found it offensive. In hindsight, I realize that I could have simply pointed to the backlash that ensued when radio personality Don Imus used the term in 2007. Part of me didn't want to have that conversation especially with a close friend. In my head I thought, "Well, he probably didn't mean any harm by it," however, I realized in that moment that not saying anything was condoning the usage of that word. I had a conversation with my friend about the word and why it can be seen as offensive. Implementing the 5-second rule into the conversation and making an effort to truly listen to my friend's point of view allowed us to have meaningful and honest dialogue about the word. He has not used the word since. I actually ended up later making a YouTube video about why the term 'nappy' is offensive and why someone calling your hair 'nappy' could be considered a microaggressive statement. Although it was a challenging conversation, it was necessary.

For more effective communication and conflict resolution, encourage your organization to implement bystander training. This type of training is focused on helping employees understand how to best intervene when they encounter bias and discrimination taking place (Miller, 2017). Bystander training teaches individuals how to recognize and address harassment and other bad behaviors when they occur in the workplace. Sharing examples with my friend of when the term nappy has been used in a derogatory way helped him to have a better understanding of why that word may be deemed offensive. We're not always going to have the answers, but the willingness to learn and engage in the conversation is what will sustain your company's DEI efforts.

Chapter Takeaways:

- The 5-second rule can be an effective way to improve listening.

- Listen to understand versus listening to respond.

- Bystander training can help employees recognize and intervene when discrimination is taking place.

CHAPTER 10

Creative Ways to Boost Inclusion

Employee Book Club

Consider spearheading an employee book club. Books, especially ones around difficult topics like race, discrimination, gender identity, sexual orientation, and things of that nature can really open a person's eyes. Your company or DEI officer may be open to sponsoring an employee book club or you can encourage employees to purchase books on their own for a monthly book club. Your organization may also consider sponsoring employee memberships to audiobook apps like Audible as an alternative to employees having to read print books. Book clubs are also a great way to help employees stay sharp, competitive and book clubs can help give your company the edge that it needs. Hosting weekly or monthly book club meetings is my recommendation.

One book that really opened my eyes was a book called *Post Traumatic Slave Syndrome* by Dr. Joy DeGruy. This book helped me understand the experiences of black people within the United States over the last few centuries. My parents immigrated to the United States from Cameroon, a country in West Africa, in the late 1980s. As a first-generation American, many of my experiences growing up in this country were not the same as my black American peers. It wasn't until high school that these disparities became apparent to me. Growing up, I sometimes felt a divide between black Americans and black Africans. The stereotypes I heard about black Americans as I grew up only made this divide in my mind grow wider. I came to the understanding that I, too, had my own biases and prejudices that had become ingrained in me.

When I read *Post Traumatic Slave Syndrome,* one of the concepts that was insightful to me was a concept of intergenerational trauma (DeAngelis, 2019). The book discussed how the trauma that slaves experienced when they were taken from Africa and brought to the United States could be passed down from generation to generation. This learned trauma impacts the experiences of black Americans today. Attributing the disadvantaged conditions and systemic inequities that black Americans face to purely internal factors does not take into consideration this intergenerational trauma perspective, which can have a severe impact on experiences and mindset. The book really helped me understand the historical context. I can be a more effective ally by understanding this concept and recognizing my own privileges. Encouraging employees to read and explore books focused on different populations will allow employees to have these same eye-opening experiences, and become more aware of their different privileges. Even as a person who would consider myself 'woke' and very culturally aware, reading this book opened my eyes. Imagine how much learning and growth can come from employees reading books from diverse perspectives. Books can do a world of change and are such a great tool for your DEI tool box.

Virtual DEI Events

Virtual events are an underutilized tool that more companies should be using. Aside from the convenience that they present, they're great because of their cost-efficiency. Virtual events are an additional way to bond outside of the workplace. After-work events can be constrictive because employees may have different familial obligations which do not afford them much free time outside of work hours. Creating virtual events is a great tool to build community among employees and offer additional ways to create a feedback loop. Following the global pandemic of Covid-19, the Diversity Dinner Dialogue was moved to an online format. To my surprise, there were still very fruitful conversations that were able to be had virtually. The breakout rooms feature that Zoom has allowed participants to talk about topics amongst themselves before reconvening with a larger group. Virtual events are advantageous because they allow employees from different parts of the country or the world to participate, whereas in-person events are limited to the particular location that the event is taking place. Being able to have perspectives from people all around the world allows for stronger, more rich conversations and insights than an in-person event.

Organizations I have worked for in the past have held employee retreats. The goal of these retreats ultimately was to create community among employees. What I've found is that these retreats typically take place annually or bi-annually. These retreats have been great opportunities to get to know my colleagues working in other departments. One thing that I suggest is to have these retreats either in a virtual setting or on a more continuous basis. Having retreats annually really does not allow you to create bonds for better understanding with your coworkers. Creating multiple employee retreats or additional opportunities to have virtual events with co-workers is a really effective way to build community. Community building is integral to DEI efforts. Networking events are a great way to build community. These events can be related to a DEI topic or they can allow you and your colleagues to forge bonds. Networking can play a vital role for career progression. One of the overarching goals of DEI efforts is to create community among employees.

Chapter Takeaways:

- Book clubs are an excellent way to boost inclusion, understanding, and belonging.

- Virtual events are an inexpensive way to create community.

- Employee events should center around creating a sense of community.

CHAPTER 11

Starting an ERG/BRG at Your Company

Employee resource groups (ERG) and business resource groups (BRG) are effective tools in your organization's DEI toolkit. ERGs/BRGs are groups established by employees who have shared characteristics. Your company can have a Muslim ERG, a black BRG, an LGBTQ+ ERG, etc. When establishing ERGs/BRGs, it is essential to figure out what the specific goals of the ERG/BRG are. Determining the specific goals will help you figure out whether an ERG/BRG will be beneficial. Both terms are used interchangeably and may be considered synonymous. Essentially ERGs/BRGs are the same thing. There is sometimes a difference in titles to convey different messages. Before establishing, assess why you want to start it in the first place. Think about what the ultimate objectives of the group will be. Create a set of goals using the S.M.A.R.T. goal-setting method, to determine what the specific goals of the ERG/BRG will be. S.M.A.R.T. is an acronym that stands for specific, measurable, achievable, relevant, and time-bound. Centering goals around this method will increase the likelihood for success.

Previously, I was a member of a women's ERG in my organization. I joined the group after receiving an email from one of my colleagues who asked me if I wanted to take part in the group. It sounded like a great idea, so I joined and I was assigned a mentor. While it was really great to meet with my mentor during the times that we were able to connect, the ultimate goal of the ERG was unclear. I understood the purpose of the mentorship was to provide a junior employee with the guidance of a senior employee, but beyond that, there should have been more specific guidelines and parameters for the partnership to be fruitful. There were no objectives or goals. When starting an ERG, it is important to have specific objectives and goals for the group to accomplish.

A few years ago, I gave a talk for an organization and afterwards I was asked a question by a white male. He shared that he was eager to join his organization's black ERG. He felt that he was an ally, and he wanted to help, however, he worried that he would not be accepted or welcomed into the group. He also didn't know how to go about joining the group. He asked me for help and advice regarding how he should go about joining. I shared with him that he should approach the ERG leader and express his desire to join. I have never seen a situation where an ERG leader prohibited someone from joining an ERG. While your ERG/BRG should definitely be a safe-space for the communities they represent, allyship is important, and the group should not prohibit anyone from joining. Excluding others defeats the purpose of the group. Members of the ERG/ BRG should have clear instructions for how to become part of the group for those who are interested.

It's important to understand that sometimes through the creation of the ERG/BRG, some members of your organization may feel excluded. This is difficult to avoid. A women's ERG, for example, may leave male employees feeling left out. The main objective of an ERG/BRG is to create community, solidarity, and allyship for employees who belong to underrepresented and marginalized groups. While anyone should be able to join your ERG/BRG, when establishing an ERG/BRG the main goal is solidarity, allyship and community-building for members of the specific group that the ERG represents. Emphasizing this as the main objective of your ERG/BRG can lessen feelings of exclusion.

ERGs/BRGs are a great way to foster inclusion in your workplace. By having a group of fellow employees to talk to who have shared characteristics and may be feeling the same way while navigating the workplace can be comforting. Having a support system is an effective way to foster employee belonging. Establishing an ERG/BRG for members of diverse groups can be impactful for your organization.

Chapter Takeaways:

- ERGs/BRGs can be instrumental in fostering more belonging and inclusion.

- Objectives and goals of the ERG/BRG should be set at the point of creation.

- To avoid feelings of exclusion, emphasize the purpose of the ERG/BRG for employees.

Case Studies

I wanted to share some common diversity, equity, and inclusion issues that I have been asked to resolve and provide recommendations for addressing these particular problems. These inquiries came from both employees and management within different organizations.

Case Study 1

Problem

An organization has a difficult time retaining black employees. There is a revolving door of black employees leaving the organization, but they do not stay for longer than one year. The manager indicates that many of these employees complain of an environment that is not welcoming or inviting to them.

Suggested Recommendation

A common issue that many organizations face is an inability to retain black employees. There are several reasons why this issue can persist. You want to ask yourself what measures are currently in place to ensure black employees, in particular, feel a sense of inclusion and belonging. Is there a black employee resource group? If not, it may be a good idea to establish one within your workplace. Also consider creating virtual and in-person events that focus on topics that are relevant to your black employees. Invite black employees to share what types of events would interest them and invite speakers to give keynotes around these specific issues.

Case Study 2

Problem

The company culture is hostile and microaggressive issues persist, according to employees.

Suggested Recommendation

You want to first enlist more information and feedback from employees that cite specific incidents. What are the main causes of a hostile work environment? Is it management? A group of employees? One particular employee? Find out the root cause(s) of the microaggressions to address the problem head-on. Implementing team-building events into your workplace can be an effective strategy to strengthen employee bonds. Training employees to better understand microaggressions and how they can impact the workplace will also be helpful. Managers should be conducting frequent check-ins with employees and teams to be able to recognize smaller issues before they develop into larger problems.

Case Study 3

Problem

Your company is struggling to attract diverse candidates for a particular role.

Suggested Recommendation

You want to first assess from where you are sourcing candidates. Think about what the demographic makeup of the colleges and universities are where you are recruiting. Instead of recruiting from solely PWIs (predominantly white institutions), think about sourcing from HBCUs (historically black colleges and universities). Also consider cultural organizations within colleges and universities. Consider the hiring and search committee and their demographic makeup. Ensure that your search committee is diverse. Implement a blind resume system so that gender, race, age and other identifiers are not displayed to increase objectivity during the hiring process.

Case Study 4

Problem

Your coworker has written something problematic and racist on their social media page.

Suggested Recommendation

With the Covid-19 pandemic, many more people worldwide will be working from home frequently and will become more reliant on the internet. Social media can be a hotbed for inappropriate behavior, and I expect these behaviors to increase. If you ever find yourself in a situation where you witness a coworker writing something you find to be offensive, it's important to have an offline or private conversation with the individual. It will resolve nothing to publicly shame someone about something they said online. If the goal is to educate someone during a teachable moment, an effective strategy is to have a conversation about the offense.

Explain your feelings and how what was written could be offensive. Sometimes people are unaware of their impact or the way a message was construed online. If you feel comfortable doing so, it's imperative to have a conversation with the individual. Understand that sometimes people will not always change, and a conversation won't always shift viewpoints or mindsets, but the alternative is silence which signals to the individual that their behavior is acceptable. Be confident and courageous with speaking out when you witness bad behaviors taking place.

Case Study 5

Problem

You witness a biased behavior taking place. The perpetrator is your manager.

Suggested Recommendation

Some people may find themselves in this tricky situation. If you ever witness your manager engaging in discriminatory behavior, there are a few courses of action you can take. Think about whether this is a first-time offense or something that has happened repeatedly. Also consider whether other people have witnessed this behavior and can corroborate what happened. Look into whether your organization has an anonymous helpline that employees can use to report harassment and other inappropriate work behaviors. Reach out to your human resource department. They are supposed to be the liaison between employees and management and should have training on how to resolve these types of issues. Although retaliation is illegal, addressing biased behavior with the offending manager could create bigger issues and could impact your job and career progression. Utilize the resources that are available to you to resolve this particular issue.

Case Study 6

Problem

Some employees have complained about your organization being biased in the way that employees are promoted.

Suggested Recommendation

A lack of objective practices and policies related to promotion can lead to inequities and disparities when it comes to who gets promoted within your organization. First examine what your promotion rates are. Does this belief actually reflect reality? If different groups are being promoted at different rates, you want to evaluate what your promotion procedures are. Are there objective criteria for how employees can get promoted and advance? Is this made apparent to employees? There should be clear criteria for how employee performance will be evaluated for promotion. Ensure equity and strengthen employee trust by being transparent with the process with employees.

Case Study 7

Problem

An employee of your organization has written something derogatory on social media about members of a particular religious community. The statement goes viral and much backlash against your organization ensues.

Suggested Recommendation

Unfortunately, this has become quite a common occurrence for organizations since the rise of social media. Most organizations have some sort of policy that outlines acceptable behavior on and off work premises. This type of behavior, if it ever occurs, should not be tolerated and should be addressed swiftly. Employees should understand the repercussions of this type of behavior. Aside from ensuring that the employee handbook contains information that outlines acceptable and unacceptable behavior, new hire training should include diversity, equity, and inclusion training where these types of behaviors are addressed. Training should be ongoing and continuous for employees.

Epilogue

You now have the tools to improve your company's DEI health. Now that you have completed this book, you have the strategies needed to:

- Understand the vital role of employee feedback in your DEI efforts

- Recognize the value of panel discussions and focus groups

- Introduce small but impactful behaviors that will increase inclusion and belonging

- Reduce microaggressive behaviors in your workplace

- Create a sense of belonging and inclusion for remote employees

- Design workshops and trainings that foster greater understanding, inclusion, and belonging

- Understand the value of the Diversity Dinner Dialogue

- Reduce misunderstandings and conflict when they arise

- Understand the role of ERGs/BRGs to drive more inclusion

Use this book as a guide as you traverse the DEI path. Understand that your DEI goals are not finite and will be constantly growing, evolving, and changing as the world changes. Thank you for trusting me to guide you on this journey and I look forward to learning more about how you've implemented the strategies detailed in this book!

References

DeAngelis, T. (2019, February). *The Legacy of Trauma.* American Psychological Association. www.apa.org/monitor/2019/02/legacy-trauma.

Miller, C.C. (2017, December 11). *Sexual Harassment Training Doesn't Work. But Some Things Do.* The New York Times. www.nytimes.com/2017/12/11/upshot/sexual -harassment-workplace-prevention-effective.html.

Phipps, S., Prieto, L.C. (2016). Tackling Micro-Aggressions in Organizations: A Broken Windows *Approach. Journal of Leadership, Accountability, and Ethics 13*(3). www.academia.edu/31568523/Tackling_Micro-

Aggressions in Organizations A Broken Win
dows Approach.

Spain, E., Groysberg, B. (2016, April). *Making Exit
Interviews Count.* Harvard Business Review.
www.hbr.org/2016/04/making-exit-interviews-
count.

The bias barrier: Allyship, inclusion, and everyday behaviors.
Deloitte. Retrieved April 24, 2020 from
www2.deloitte.com/us/en/pages/about-
deloitte/articles/inclusion-insights.html.

Twaronite, K. (2019, May 11) *Five Findings on the
Importance of Belonging.* EY.
www.ey.com/en_us/diversity-inclusiveness/ey-
belonging-barometer-workplace-study.

Dear Reader,

I appreciate you taking the time to read this book and hope that you will use what you have learned to help you improve your corporate diversity efforts. As a thank you to you for picking up this book, I would like to offer you a free checklist of *10 ways to improve your diversity, equity, and inclusion efforts right now.* The checklist can be found at www.drjanicegassam.com/juneteenth by entering the promo code juneteenth.

By securing your free checklist, you will be added to the mailing list and you will receive free information to help you improve your company's DEI efforts. You will also receive updates about upcoming in-person and virtual Diversity Dinner Dialogues and other events.

Claim your checklist today!

Looking forward to keeping in touch!"

Kind Regards,

Janice Z. Gassam

About the Author

Janice Z. (Gassam) Asare is a consultant, who created BWG Business Solutions, LLC. The purpose of BWG Business Solutions, LLC is to help organizations create environments that are equitable for all employees. Janice facilitates workshops and delivers keynote speeches and "Awareness Talks" to spark important dialogue and develop strategies for more workplace inclusion. She is the host of the Diversity Dinner Dialogue in New York City, which are free workshops on diversity, equity, and inclusion-related issues that companies and individuals are facing. She is a senior contributing writer for Forbes.com, having authored nearly 200 articles and a contributing writer for *Fast Company*. Janice is a TEDx speaker, having delivered a talk on emotional intelligence. Janice has a Ph.D. in Organizational Psychology, and she is a professor of Business Management at Sacred Heart University. In February 2020 Janice started a podcast, "Dirty Diversity" where she discusses all things diversity, equity and inclusion (or lack thereof). Janice volunteers as a job coach for the Coalition for the Homeless, where she helps women with job preparedness, resume-writing, and cover letter reviews. She also serves as a director for her local Toastmasters chapter. She resides in the Greater New York City area with her husband.